D1124601

Friends
of the
Danville Library

This item is a gift
from the

Friends of the Danville Library

BLUE BANNER BIOGRAPHY

Nicki
MINAJ

Joanne Mattern

Mitchell Lane
PUBLISHERS
P.O. Box 196
Hockessin, Delaware 19707
Visit us on the web: www.mitchelllane.com
Comments? Email us: mitchelllane@mitchelllane.com

Mitchell Lane
PUBLISHERS

Printing   1   2   3   4   5   6   7   8   9

Blue Banner Biographies

Abby Wambach	Ice Cube	Miguel Tejada
Adele	Ja Rule	Mike Trout
Alicia Keys	Jamie Foxx	Nancy Pelosi
Allen Iverson	Jay-Z	Natasha Bedingfield
Ashanti	Jennifer Hudson	Nicki Minaj
Ashlee Simpson	Jennifer Lopez	One Direction
Ashton Kutcher	Jessica Simpson	Orianthi
Avril Lavigne	J. K. Rowling	Orlando Bloom
Blake Lively	John Legend	P. Diddy
Bow Wow	Justin Berfield	Peyton Manning
Brett Favre	Justin Timberlake	Prince William
Britney Spears	Kanye West	Queen Latifah
Bruno Mars	Kate Hudson	Robert Downey Jr.
CC Sabathia	Katy Perry	Ron Howard
Carrie Underwood	Keith Urban	Sean Kingston
Chris Brown	Kelly Clarkson	Shakira
Chris Daughtry	Kenny Chesney	Shia LaBeouf
Christina Aguilera	Ke$ha	Shontelle Layne
Clay Aiken	Kevin Durant	Soulja Boy Tell 'Em
Cole Hamels	Kristen Stewart	Stephenie Meyer
Condoleezza Rice	Lady Gaga	Taylor Swift
Corbin Bleu	Lance Armstrong	T.I.
Daniel Radcliffe	Leona Lewis	Timbaland
David Ortiz	Lionel Messi	Tim McGraw
David Wright	Lindsay Lohan	Tim Tebow
Derek Jeter	LL Cool J	Toby Keith
Drew Brees	Ludacris	Usher
Eminem	Mariah Carey	Vanessa Anne Hudgens
Eve	Mario	Will.i.am
Fergie	Mary J. Blige	Zac Efron
Flo Rida	Mary-Kate and Ashley Olsen	
Gwen Stefani	Megan Fox	

Library of Congress Cataloging-in-Publication Data
Mattern, Joanne, 1963–
Nicki Minaj / by Joanne Mattern.
   pages cm
Includes bibliographical references and index.
ISBN 978-1-61228-468-2 (library bound)
1. Minaj, Nicki—Juvenile literature. 2. Rap musicians—United States—Biography—Juvenile literature. 3. Hip-hop—United States—Juvenile literature. I. Title.
ML3930.M64M38 2013
782.421649092—dc23
[B]
                                                 2013023041
eBook ISBN: 9781612285252

ABOUT THE AUTHOR: Joanne Mattern has written many nonfiction books for children. She grew up listening to all types of music and remains a big fan of music today, so some of her favorite books are biographies of musical artists. Previous biographies for Mitchell Lane include *Benny Goodman, Count Basie, One Direction, Jennifer Hudson, the Jonas Brothers, Ludacris,* and *Selena.* Joanne lives with her husband, four children, and several pets in New York State.

Blue Banner Biography

Fans adore Nicki Minaj's live performances, such as this 2011 concert at New York City's Central Park.

An Important Decision

Onika "Nicki" Maraj was feeling discouraged. She had graduated from high school with plans to become an actress. However, no one seemed interested in giving the outspoken young woman an acting job after she graduated. Instead, she had worked at a series of jobs that she really hated. Nicki worked as a waitress in restaurants and also worked in offices, but she had a hard time getting along with people. Nicki was a nice person, but she often got annoyed dealing with people, especially if they were not nice to her. She often talked back to people and swore at them. Once she even chased after a customer who made her angry!

Nicki worked all day to pay her rent and expenses, but her heart was not in her job. After a short while, she realized she did not even want to be an actress anymore. What Nicki really wanted to do was be a rapper. She often got in trouble for making phone calls at work. These calls were to music producers or anyone else Nicki felt could get her noticed. After work, Nicki stayed up late writing raps and recording music. It didn't take long before Nicki's boss at her office job had had enough. One day, he fired Nicki.

Nicki did not know what to do. She knew the practical thing would be to find another job so she could pay her bills. But Nicki knew that would not make her happy and she would probably end up being fired again. Also, if she had a job she hated, she would not be able to concentrate on her true love, which was music.

Eventually Nicki stopped looking for a job. She threw herself into making music. For the next few months, Nicki did nothing but study music, listen to songs, write raps, and record songs. She did everything she could to get better. Nicki knew that she had to make music her full-time project, even if she never made any money doing it. More than anything, she wanted to be successful. But she knew she could only be successful if she did things her way.

A Tough Childhood

*O*nika Tanya Maraj was born on December 8, 1982, in Saint James, near the capital city of Port of Spain, Trinidad. Trinidad is part of the nation of Trinidad and Tobago, a group of islands in the Caribbean Sea. They are located just off the northeastern coast of South America. Onika was always called Nicki by her family. And that family was very large. Nicki's mother, Carol, had five brothers and sisters and many nieces and nephews too. Carol's mother was the head of the family. Nicki and her older brother, Jelani, grew up among this extended family.

When Nicki was three years old, her mother and father, Robert, moved to the United States. They wanted to find jobs and a better life there. Nicki and Jelani were left behind in the care of their grandmother. This situation was not unusual for that time and place. "A lot of times, when you're from the islands, your parents leave and then send for you because it's easier when they have . . . a place to stay, when they have a job," Nicki explained on MTV many years later.

Nicki didn't mind living with her grandmother and other family members, even though their living conditions were crowded. "Growing up in Trinidad, I didn't know that we were poor," Nicki later explained in an *E!* television special. "Ten people living in a three-bedroom home and all the dogs and cats my grandmother had, none of that seemed really abnormal." However, Nicki really missed her parents. The little girl had hoped they would come back for her right away. Instead, Nicki did not see her mother and father for two years.

Finally, Nicki received wonderful news. Her parents sent money for her and Jelani to come live with them in New York City. Nicki was very excited . . . until she got off the plane. It was winter and New York was cold and snowy. The family's house was even more disappointing. Nicki had imagined that everyone in the United States was rich and lived in beautiful houses. Instead, her new home in South Jamaica, Queens, was poor and shabby.

> **Nicki had imagined that everyone in the United States was rich and lived in beautiful houses.**

In spite of the disappointing living conditions, Nicki was happy to be back with her mother. However, she was not as happy to see her father. Robert had a job working for a credit card company, but he lost it after a short time. When that happened, Robert became an alcoholic and a drug addict. At that time, crack cocaine was a huge problem in New York City. Nicki's father was so desperate for drugs that he often sold the family's furniture and other possessions. Even worse, he became violent. Nicki and Jelani frequently heard Robert screaming at their mother. If he got really angry, he would punch holes in the walls.

One night, Carol was so worried about her husband's behavior that she sent the children to a neighbor's house to sleep. During that night, Robert burned down the house. Carol was almost killed in the fire. Nicki lost nearly everything she had. As she explained to Siobhan O'Connor of *Vibe*, "All my dolls, all my stuffed animals, all my pictures were burnt. I was one of those kids that kept all that stuff. I cared a lot." Nicki later wrote about this terrible night in a song called "Autobiography."

Although Nicki was afraid of her father, she loved her mother very much. Carol worked as a nurse's aide to support the family. She brought Nicki and Jelani to church so they could find positive values. Another gift Carol gave her daughter was music. The radio was always on in their house. Nicki grew up listening to pop music. Some of her favorite singers were Whitney Houston, Madonna, and Cyndi Lauper.

Nicki also loved to read. She had a vivid imagination and liked to create stories about herself. Sometimes she spoke with funny accents or dressed in unusual clothes to pretend she was someone else. Most of all,

Nicki dreamed of a better life. Years later, she told *USA Today* that she remembered "kneeling at the foot of my mother's bed every morning, saying, 'Please, God, make me rich and famous so that I can take care of her.'" Nicki's mother and grandmother watched a lot of soap operas, so Nicki decided she would become a soap opera star and make a lot of money. "Then my mother and brother and me could sneak away and my father would never find us," she decided. Although Nicki did not become a soap opera star, she soon discovered she had a talent for another way to entertain people.

Nicki Minaj dreamt of a better life where she made a lot of money. "Then my mother and brother and me could sneak away and my father would never find us."

Fighting for a Chance

Nicki enjoyed school, especially her music and drama classes. When she was a fifth grader, she had a teacher who encouraged Nicki and her classmates to be creative. The class wrote and acted out plays that were based on their own experiences. This support helped Nicki believe in herself and think that she could have a career in the arts. Later, Nicki joined the school band and learned to play the clarinet.

By this time, Nicki had also discovered hip-hop music. This type of music was very popular in Queens. Several major hip-hop stars, including 50 Cent and Ja Rule, came from Nicki's own neighborhood of South Jamaica. Nicki started writing rhymes and rapping when she was eleven years old. She wrote about topics she was familiar with, such as friendship, school, and even eating cookies. Other children in the neighborhood enjoyed Nicki's raps. Their enjoyment encouraged her to perform even more.

By the time she started high school, Nicki knew that she wanted a career in the performing arts. So one day she and her mother traveled to Manhattan, another part of New

York City, to audition for the Fiorello H. LaGuardia High School of Music & Art and the Performing Arts. This school had been made famous by the hit movie and TV series *Fame*. Because she loved music, she tried out for the music department. Unfortunately, Nicki's voice was hoarse that day and clearly not at its best, and the school turned her down.

"I knew I'd flunked miserably," Nicki told Siobhan O'Connor. "I was crying and embarrassed and I didn't want anyone in the school to see me. I just wanted to go home."

Nicki's mother said no. She ordered her daughter to try out for the school's drama department. When Nicki saw other students performing, she realized she was in the right place. Her audition went well and she was accepted into the school's drama department.

Nicki felt right at home at LaGuardia. For the first time, she was meeting other people who enjoyed pretending to be someone else. People did whatever they could in order to get noticed. They wore crazy outfits, just like Nicki enjoyed doing. As one of her classmates explained to Siobhan O'Connor, "You could tell at LaGuardia what someone's major was based on their behavior, and Nicki was definitely a drama major." Nicki felt confident and talented.

> "I went to my mother and said, 'Look, I'm not going back to work.' I'd been fired like fifteen times because I had a horrible attitude."

However, things changed after Nicki's graduation. Although she made contacts with several talent agents, Nicki's only acting job was in an off-Broadway play that very few people saw, called *In Case You Forget*. Instead, she ended up working as a waitress in Red Lobster, a seafood restaurant. Nicki was a terrible waitress. Instead of being nice to customers, Nicki told them exactly what she thought. Once one of her super-long nails broke off and plopped into a customer's salad. Nicki thought it was funny. Her boss didn't. He did not appreciate Nicki's attitude and she was soon fired. Nicki got a job in another restaurant, but she was fired from that job as well.

Nicki went on to work at many different jobs over the next few years, and she was fired from all of them. In a 2010 interview with *Billboard* magazine, she recalled, "The last job I had was as an office manager in a little, tiny room where I literally wanted to strangle this guy because he was so loud and obnoxious. I would go home with stress pains in my neck and my back. That's when I went to my mother and said, 'Look, I'm not going back to work.' I'd been fired like fifteen times because I had a horrible attitude."

Instead of looking for a new job, Nicki decided to focus on her first love: music. She decided that if she was going to succeed, she would not let anyone tell her what to do. Nicki wanted to be in control of everything about her music. She spent all day and night writing and recording original songs. She also set up meetings with music executives. Nicki made mixtapes of her music and played them for anyone who would listen. These tapes were actually CDs that were not released by major record labels but became popular through word of mouth. Nicki wanted to succeed, not just for herself, but for her family.

Wearing a typically outrageous outfit, Minaj and her friend Safaree "SB" Samuels head to the taping of a TV show in London, England.

Finally, in 2002, Nicki was asked to join a New York City rap group called the Hood$tars. Nicki became close friends with a member of the group, Safaree "SB" Samuels. Samuels would go on to become one of Nicki's closest advisors. Another member of the group was the son of an industry professional, Lucien George Jr., who was known as Bowlegged Lou. Bowlegged Lou believed in Nicki and tried to get her signed to a record label. However, no one at that time believed a female rap singer could be successful.

Nicki decided not to worry about getting a record contract. She took matters into her own hands and uploaded her photos and music to a website called MySpace. Nicki also began performing in small clubs in New York City. Many of the people who came to her shows had seen her videos. Word of Nicki's talent began to spread.

One day, a music executive named Fendi happened to see Nicki's MySpace page. When her music came on, he was amazed. In an interview with the website NCHipHopConnect.com, Fendi recalled, "I'm like, 'who is this? This can't be a [woman]. This music sounds hard.'" Fendi arranged a meeting with Nicki and signed her to his record label, Dirty Money Records. He also convinced Nicki to change her last name from Maraj to Minaj.

Nicki began to get noticed in the hip-hop community. She appeared in a magazine-styled DVD called *The Come Up* that featured interviews and music from up-and-coming hip-hop artists. Nicki didn't know it, but a video she performed on one of these DVDs would change her life.

> *Nicki appeared in a magazine-styled DVD called* The Come Up *that featured interviews and music from up-and-coming hip-hop artists.*

CHAPTER 4

Nicki Hits the Big Time

*F*or years, Nicki had been a huge fan of rapper Lil Wayne. Lil Wayne had several top-selling albums. In 2005, he released *Tha Carter II*, which sold more than two million copies and rose to Number 2 on the *Billboard* 200 Album chart. Fendi interviewed Lil Wayne for *The Come Up*. Then he decided to film Nicki freestyling, or making up her own rap, to one of Lil Wayne's songs and added her performance to the DVD magazine. Lil Wayne saw the video and got very excited. He told Fendi he wanted to meet Nicki right away. In addition to being a rapper, Lil Wayne was president of a company called Cash Money Records and had his own label there, called Young Money. Soon after he met Nicki, he signed her to a contract with his record company.

Nicki moved to Atlanta, Georgia, and began appearing in clubs. She also released a number of mixtapes. Nicki's style of rap was hard and tough. She often rapped about sex and violence. Nicki did this so men in the hip-hop industry would take her seriously. "I always wanted to play with the boys," she said. "I didn't want to . . . have a

Nicki Minaj performs with her idol and mentor, rap star Lil Wayne, at the 2013 Billboard Music Awards in Las Vegas.

sidekick role. I wanted to be more of a lead character—a superhero." This approach was very unusual at that time. Nicki also used different voices and accents on her CDs. She mixed singing with clever wordplay, and often spoke in a rapid-fire way that was hard to understand at first.

In 2008, Lil Wayne went on a very successful tour. Nicki went with him. Touring with Lil Wayne introduced Nicki to a much larger audience. In 2009, she released her newest mixtape, *Beam Me Up Scotty*. The CD was featured on MTV's *Mixtape Daily* show. One of the songs, "I Go Crazy," featured Lil Wayne. This song received a lot of radio airplay and hit Number 20 on the *Billboard* Hot Rap Songs chart.

Later that year, Nicki appeared on Lil Wayne's album, *We Are Young Money*, which showcased many of the artists on his Young Money label. Nicki rapped on one of the songs on the album, "Bedrock." The song became a huge hit and raced to Number 2 on the *Billboard* Hot 100 chart. Suddenly everyone wanted to know more about that female rapper with the crazy style!

Over the next year, Nicki sang with many famous performers, including Rihanna, Christina Aguilera, Usher, Robin Thicke, and Kanye West. When industry veteran Rick Ross saw Nicki working with West, who was one of the biggest names in hip-hop, he was very impressed. "Before that day she was a great entertainer, but for me to get in the studio with my own two eyes and see her write her verse, I knew that was gonna be one of the greatest voices of the year," he told the website Rap-Up.com.

In June 2010, Nicki's song "Your Love" became the number one song on *Billboard's* Hot Rap Songs chart and stayed there for eight weeks. Nicki became the first female rapper in eight years to have a number one hit. Only Lil' Kim and Missy Elliott had achieved this milestone before Nicki. Nicki released several more hits. By October 2010, she achieved another record. Nicki had the most singles on *Billboard's* Hot 100 chart at any one time.

In November 2010, Nicki finally released her first album. It was called *Pink Friday*. The album was a huge success. For the first time, fans could hear Nicki rapping and singing on her own instead of just appearing with other artists. Of course, Nicki continued to work with other hip-hop stars. One of the most popular songs on *Pink Friday* was "Moment 4 Life," which featured an artist named Drake. Drake would go on to become a major hip-hop star and a close friend of Nicki's. Another huge song was "Super Bass," which became one of Nicki's biggest hits. *Pink Friday* went on to hit Number 1 on the *Billboard* charts and sold more than four million digital copies.

"Moment 4 Life" also showed off Nicki's acting skills. On that song, she introduced some imaginary characters,

Madonna performs with Nicki and M.I.A. during the halftime show of Super Bowl XLVI on February 5, 2012. Nicki was thrilled to perform with Madonna, who had been one of her favorite singers when she was growing up.

including Martha, the fairy godmother, and Martha's son, Roman. Roman would go on to become one of Nicki's best-known characters. Nicki also played the part of Barbie, like the Barbie doll popular with children. People loved the character and Nicki began calling her fans "Barbz."

Nicki hit another career high in 2011, when she got to work with one of her idols, Madonna. Madonna invited Nicki and M.I.A., another female hip-hop singer, to perform on a song called "Give Me All Your Luvin'." Two months later, on February 5, 2012, the three women performed the song during the halftime show at the Super Bowl. More than 114 million people around the world saw the performance. Nicki's career had reached new heights.

CHAPTER 5

New Horizons

*A*t the Grammy Awards just one week after the Super Bowl, Nicki performed a song called "Roman Holiday," from her new album, *Pink Friday: Roman Reloaded*. The song was part of a longer dramatic performance called *The Exorcism of Roman*. It was the first time the ceremony had featured a solo female rap singer. Many viewers hated the performance and found it dark and disturbing. Other people thought the performance was exciting. Whatever their reaction, Nicki's performance got everyone talking. Nicki also performed to honor the memory of one of her idols, Whitney Houston, who had died suddenly and unexpectedly the day before the show.

In 2012, the popular TV show *American Idol* announced that Nicki would be one of the judges for the 2013 season. She joined original judge Randy Jackson and two new judges, Mariah Carey and country star Keith Urban. Although Nicki and Mariah Carey had worked together before, they did not get along well on the show. The two even fought on the air. *American Idol* producers had hoped that the new judges would help increase the ratings for the show, but the season turned out to be a failure. Many people disliked the new judges, especially Nicki. Nicki never responded to comments from gossip magazines or Internet postings. However, the entire team of judges was let go at the end of the season.

Nicki also became known for her fashion and appearance, not just her music. Nicki had always enjoyed changing her hair and her clothes to reflect different characters. Once, when a neighbor asked why she had done something unusual to her hair, Nicki replied, "I'm someone new in this hair." Nicki especially loves bright colors.

Nicki with fellow American Idol judges Keith Urban and Randy Jackson, and former contestant Hailey Reinhart in May 2013. Nicki only lasted one year as a judge on the show.

Nicki's performance at the 2012 Grammy Awards was both disturbing and exciting, and it left millions of people talking about her dramatic style.

Nicki's actual hair is short and dark, but she always wears wigs in public. Wigs help her save time when she is getting ready for an appearance and also keep her from permanently damaging her hair. Nicki has also said she gets bored easily and that is why she wears so many different and very outrageous outfits. Nicki's influence on fashion has become so great that she has appeared at New York's famous Fashion Week, where designers launch their new collections.

Nicki is also a very smart businesswomen. She has given her name and style to nail colors, makeup, and perfume, and may soon launch her own clothing line. Nicki wants to be more than just a hip-hop artist. She told Complex Media, "I am the marketer and promoter of the Nicki Minaj brand."

The Nicki Minaj brand is also about giving back. Nicki knows she has been very fortunate and she is eager to share her good fortune with others. Nicki was part of a charity auction run by Charitybuzz.com to benefit HIV/AIDS patients. In 2011, the Mattel toy company created a Nicki Minaj Barbie doll, which was auctioned off for more than $15,000. "It's just a one of a kind, limited edition for charity, and so I never thought Mattel would even pay attention to me," she happily said at *Billboard*'s

Women in Music event in December 2011. "For me this is a very major moment, because it just shows that you can come from nothing and still be a force in the main world, a business woman, and hopefully a mogul one day." The following year, Nicki worked with Give Back Brands to create a perfume, with part of the sales going to charity.

One of Nicki's biggest joys has been making a childhood promise come true. She was able to buy her mother a house. "I got her the house I always wanted to live in when I was a kid," she said in an interview with *Allure*

Nicki was thrilled when the Mattel toy company created a one-of-a-kind Barbie doll in her image. The doll was auctioned off for charity and raised $15,000.

magazine. "I finally could breathe a sigh of relief. . . . The one thing I had been driving toward was buying my mom a home." Nicki is also working to repair her relationship with her father, who stopped using drugs and alcohol.

> "I want to show little girls that the possibilities are endless. That's my goal—to not only do it for myself, but to show them I can do whatever I put my mind to."

Nicki Minaj is a great success story. She always refused to act in the ways that other people expected her to. Instead she went ahead and succeeded by following her own rules. Nicki is happy to be a role model for others, especially young girls. In 2012, she told England's *Guardian* newspaper, "I want to show little girls that the possibilities are endless. That's my goal—to not only do it for myself, but to show them I can do whatever I put my mind to."

Nicki has succeeded beyond her wildest dreams.

1982 Onika "Nicki" Maraj is born in Trinidad on December 8.

1985 Nicki's parents move to the United States, leaving Nicki and her brother with their grandmother.

1987 Nicki and her brother move to Queens, New York.

2001 Nicki graduates from New York's Fiorello H. LaGuardia High School of Music & Art and the Performing Arts; appears in off-Broadway play *In Case You Forget*.

2002 Nicki joins the Hood$tars.

2004 Nicki signs with Dirty Money Records; she changes her name to Nicki Minaj.

2005 Nicki meets Lil Wayne, who signs her to his Young Money label.

2008 Nicki tours with Lil Wayne.

2009 Nicki releases her mixtape *Beam Me Up Scotty* and has her first hit on the Billboard charts.

2010 Nicki becomes the first female rapper in eight years to hit number one on the *Billboard* chart with her song "Your Love"; later that year she has the most singles on *Billboard*'s Hot 100 chart at any one time; Nicki releases *Pink Friday*, which includes the hit "Super Bass."

2011 Nicki records with Madonna and M.I.A.

2012 Nicki appears with Madonna and M.I.A. at the Super Bowl halftime show; she appears at the Grammys.

2013 Nicki appears as a judge on the 12th season of *American Idol*.

Pink Friday (2010)
Pink Friday: Roman Reloaded (2012)

AWARDS

2010   **BET Awards**
Best Female Hip-Hop Artist
Best New Artist
BET Hip-Hop Awards
People's Champ Award
Rookie of the Year
Made-You-Look Award (Best Hip-Hop Style)

2011   **American Music Awards**
Favorite Rap/Hip-Hop Artist
Favorite Rap/Hip-Hop Album (Pink Friday)

BET Awards
Best Female Hip-Hop Artist

BET Hip-Hop Awards
Made-You-Look Award (Best Hip-Hop Style)
MVP of the Year

MTV Video Music Awards
Best Hip-Hop Video ("Super Bass")

Soul Train Music Awards
Best Hip-Hop Song of the Year ("Moment 4
Life")

2012   **BET Awards**
Best Female Hip-Hop Artist
Billboard Music Awards
Top Streaming Song (Video) ("Super Bass")

MTV Video Music Awards
Best Female Video

Teen Choice Awards
Choice R&B/Hip-Hop Song
("Starships")
Choice R&B/Hip-Hop Artist

FURTHER READING

Find Out More

Boyd, Christie Brewer. *Nicki Minaj*. Farmington Hills, Mich.: Lucent Books, 2013.

Britton, Felicity. *Nicki Minaj: Conquering Hip-Hop*. Minneapolis: Twenty-First Century Books, 2013.

Harris, Ashley Rae. *Nicki Minaj: Rapper & Fashion Star*. Minneapolis: ABDO Publishers, 2013.

"Ten Questions for Nicki Minaj." *Teen Vogue*, April 2011. http://www.teenvogue.com/celebrity-style/2011-04/nicki-minaj-interview/?slide=1

Works Consulted

Concepcion, Mariel. "Nicki Minaj: The Billboard Cover Story." *Billboard*, Novmber 12, 2010. http://www.billboard.com/articles/news/951113/nicki-minaj-the-billboard-cover-story

"E Special: Nicki Minaj." E! Entertainment, July 12, 2011. http://www.eonline.com/videos/E_Special_Nicki_Minaj/167166

Gardner, Elysa. "Nicki Minaj Brings Her Theatrical Style to *Pink Friday*." *USA Today*, November 23, 2013.

God-Meta, "Always Been a Businessman: Interview with Hip-Hop Mogul Fendi." NCHipHopConnect.com, October 6, 2010. http://www.nchiphopconnect.com/fendi10510.php

Harris, Isoul. *Nicki Minaj: Hip Pop Moments 4 Life*. London: Omnibus Press, 2013.

Hattenstone, Simon. "Nicki Minaj: I Have Bigger Balls Than the Boys." The *Guardian*, April 27, 2012. http://m.guardian.co.uk/ms/p/gnm/op/view.m?id=15&gid=/music/2012/apr/27/nicki-minaj-bigger-balls-than-the-boys&cat=music

Minaj, Nicki. "Give Back Brands Signs Exclusive Fragrance." MyPinkFriday, April 23, 2013. http://mypinkfriday.com/news/73601

Newman, Judith. "Just Try to Look Away." *Allure*, April 2012,
    p. 236.
"Nicki Minaj: My Time Now." MTV.com, November 28, 2010.
    http://www.mtv.com/shows/nicki_minaj_my_time_
    now/series.jhtml
"Nicki Minaj: Self-Possessed." Complex Media, March 20,
    2012. http://www.complex.com/music/2012/03/
    nicki-minaj-cover-story
O'Connor, Siobhan. "Character Study: Just How Real is Nicki
    Minaj?" *Vibe*, June 23, 2010. http://www.vibe.com/article/
    character-study-just-how-real-nicki-minaj-cover-story
"Rick Ross Says 'Monster' Made Him a Nicki Minaj Believer."
    Rap-Up.com, September 16, 2010. http://www.rap-up.
    com/2010/09/16/rap-up-tv-rick-ross-says-monster-made-
    him-a-nicki-minaj-believer/
Schneider, Marc. "Nicki Minaj: Barbie Doll a 'Very Major
    Moment' for Me." *Billboard*, December 2, 2011.
    http://www.billboard.com/articles/news/464862/
    nicki-minaj-barbie-doll-a-very-major-moment-for-me

On the Internet

American Idol
    http://american idol.com
MTV
    http://www.mtv.com/artists/nicki-minaj/
My Pink Friday
    http://www.MyPinkFriday.com

INDEX